JUDGES POSTCARDS
A brief history

There is every chance that the postcard you send home from your holiday started life in Sussex. Since 1902 Hastings has been the home of Judges, one of Britain's leading publishers of quality picture postcards.

When Fred Judge arrived in Hastings in 1902 he could have had little idea of the worldwide impact he was to make on the business of postcard publishing. But Fred was a master with a camera and a natural entrepreneur. Fred Judge was born in Yorkshire in 1872. Photography was always his real interest, and it was while visiting Sussex in 1902 that he made the decision to give up engineering for a career as a photographer.

Fred and his brother Thomas purchased an existing business in Hastings and set up as photographers and photographic dealers under the name of Judge's Photo Stores. Although the idea of sending an illustrated card through the post was not new (the first having appeared towards the end of the nineteenth century) Fred made his mark by setting himself extremely high artistic standards. At first he concentrated on local scenes and activities. Having taken his pictures he would go straight back to the darkroom to make them into postcards – often for sale within a few hours; and the quality of his work was such that passers by would gather outside the shop window for a sight of his latest work.

Technically stunning, and using all the latest photographic technology, Fred's pictures won over 100 medals, and one-man exhibitions of his work were held in London, Washington, New York and Tokyo.

Back in Hastings the business was expanding, necessitating moves to bigger and better premises, culminating in the move in 1927 to the purpose-built factory that the company occupies to this day. Although the building has been developed and extended, the Italianate façade remains a famous landmark on the A259 coast road.

Fred Judge died in February 1950 at the age of 78, having built up an internationally respected company. The business was sold to another Judges photographer, who introduced lithographic colour printing. Then in 1984 Judges became a real family concern once again when Bernard and Jan Wolford took over. It became even more of a family business when their son Graeme, now managing director, joined, followed by Trevor, now sales director. The present management can truly be said to be building on the foundations laid by Fred Judge over ninety years ago.

Judges Postcards Ltd, 176 Bexhill Road, St Leonards on Sea,
East Sussex, TN38 8BN
Tel: 01424 420919; Fax: 01424 438538
www.judges.co.uk

SURREY
IN OLD PHOTOGRAPHS

DAVE RANDLE
FROM THE JUDGES POSTCARD ARCHIVE COLLECTION

SUTTON PUBLISHING

Sutton Publishing Limited
Phoenix Mill · Thrupp · Stroud
Gloucestershire · GL5 2BU

First published 2003

British Library Cataloguing in Publication Data
A catalogue record for this book is available from
the British Library.

ISBN 0-7509-3383-6

Typeset in 11/13.5 Sabon.
Typesetting and origination by
Sutton Publishing Limited.
Printed and bound in England by
J.H. Haynes & Co. Ltd, Sparkford.

Introduction

Although largely rural, the county of Surrey's destiny is intimately associated with that of London. Until the middle ages most of South London was part of Surrey – including Holborn, Lambeth and Southwark. Five hundred years later much of northern Surrey is now part of London.

The relationship has seen the county benefit from the wealth and power of both church and state, while the capital's aristocrats and high clergy gained from the proximity of ideal country seats and hunting grounds.

And the symbiosis is not solely political. Surrey's historical and geographical development is owed in great part to the presence of the mighty River Thames at its northerly border. That river and the city that bounds it are dependent upon the tributaries that flow into it from the Surrey uplands – the Tolkienish-sounding Wandle, the Mole and the Wey.

The hobbit-master's characters would not be out of place here. Even today Surrey conveys a sense that, at heart, it never really ceased to be a Saxon kingdom, its warriors just getting in a few rounds of golf while they await the return of the king. Dorking, Godalming, Haslemere – the descriptive place names in one of the most poetic of ancient tongues evoke a landscape in which every leaf, stream, tree, rock or blade of grass had a value and a unique place. Many people lived out their entire lives in a few acres of land so they were able to know it intimately. Their tiny world was a huge store of wonders that modern man would pass by in a sealed-up car with the stereo playing.

Because of its Saxon heritage, Surrey has retained that sense of farmstead insularity. Topographical features, man's interrelationship with his environment – even a record of things long gone – the county's story is kept alive by that language.

The Weald – the once almost impenetrable southern woodland that also covered much of Kent and Sussex – exists now mainly in name only. But that name describes a nature all its own – separate from the Norman 'forests', set up and managed for les toffs to go hunting in – the cradle of industries that could only grow from that nature: the 'Wealden' iron workings, paper, cloth and gunpowder mills.

For all this, it was in Norman times that the county began to be much developed beyond the fringes of London. Farnham and Guildford became strongholds under the latest wave of invaders whose alignment was more toward their homeland to the south. More traffic passed this way en route to and from France than had previously been normal and the Norman barons were understandably keen to do in Surrey what people from the Home Counties are now doing in northern France – grab a piece of unspoilt countryside for themselves. Although the conquerors were soon assimilated throughout the land, the south-eastern corner of England inevitably held special attractions.

It is especially fitting then that the document that changed the course of history, Magna Carta, should have been ratified in Surrey. On 15 June 1215 King John, sundry nobles, ecclesiastical types and freemen from the various boroughs gathered on the little island in the Thames. Never a popular monarch, by this time John had not only alienated most of his subjects, but actually lost most of his lands to the barons. The bluffer barons from the north had it in mind to take the rest, but a Godalming man, Archbishop Stephen Langton, managed to persuade them to include lesser nobles and the common folk in the new deal.

The rest – like that bit – is history. Ordinary people had rights for the first time. The divine right of kings to give their subjects grief was curtailed (at least to some extent). The foundations were laid for later bills of rights, such as that of the United States, which draws heavily on Magna Carta. And Archbishop Langton had a pub named after him.

Over a period of time the land settled into the more peaceful version of the Norman model, worshipping in Norman churches and paying fealty to Norman lords of the manor. The greater part of the county was involved in pastoral activities, while the northern fringe became more and more a dormitory or a resort from the squalor and horrors of London. Even Henry VIII built himself a place near Epsom.

The peculiarly English practice of expelling beggars from the capital inspired a boom in highway robbery on the commons and heaths to the south of the Thames during the seventeenth and eighteenth centuries. During the heyday of the mail coaches people travelled more and further, so that by this time there was regular traffic between Portsmouth and London crossing the county – as well as that from Salisbury or Exeter. As the network of coach roads expanded, the highwaymen grew with it until armed troopers were demanded.

William Cobbett, author of *Rural Rides*, was born at Farnham. He had no doubt that London was a bad influence. But just as Surrey benefited from royal patronage in the past, it is equally well placed in these more democratic times to share in the wealth generated by the capital. The so-called 'stockbroker belt' has been a long-time beneficiary. Pubs, gardens, stately homes and other tourist attractions throughout this comparatively small county have a huge customer base on hand to bring wealth to the county at short notice.

A lot of the major changes in Surrey life have taken place in recent years. The M25 and M3; the absorption of Croydon and Sutton into Greater London; the shift of emphasis from Kingston to Guildford, all are twentieth-century upheavals, not yet flat history, but living memory.

This first selection of photographs from the Judges Postcards archive covers that century. The majority of these images have not been seen for a long time, so they should bring back memories for many, and new light for others.

Because they are from the recent past, they will bring the rosy glow of nostalgia. However they are looked at they are a valuable addition to our record and understanding.

SURREY
IN OLD PHOTOGRAPHS

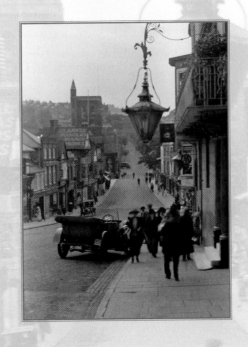

The Clock House from the opposite angle, sixty years on. Little had changed then – and little has now. There is still a very pleasant tea room, but there's a good deal more traffic.

Opposite: Already maturing nicely, The Clock House at Abinger Hammer was less than twenty years old when this picture was taken. The village's name comes from the heyday of the local iron industry when what are now watercress beds were 'hammerponds'.

The name Banstead refers to its suitability to the growing of beans, though it was known equally for the production of mint in olden times. Its commons, a number of which remain, were also ideal for grazing sheep. This is the Victoria Inn with a new neighbour in the 1980s.

This is a view of nearby Brockham Green from Christ Church after a snowfall in the early 1970s.

Opposite: St Michael's church at Betchworth in the 1920s, prior to the controversial rebuilding of the tower in 1963 with ashlared Portland stone.

The Elim Bible College was founded in Clapham in 1925. Forty years later it moved here to Capel, between Dorking and Horsham. This photograph was taken in 1970, when the buildings here were still coping with student numbers. In 1987 the college moved to Nantwich in Cheshire where it is now known as Regents Theological College. Fittingly, the name 'Capel', which also occurs elsewhere, derives from chapel.

Opposite: Camberley grew up from the old York Town Gate of the Army Staff College, which opened here in 1862. In the late 1990s the college was briefly abandoned, while army training was combined with that for the Navy and Air Force. Now it is used for Army Management Consultancy, Accountancy and Medico-legal departments.

The smart new Harvey's store in Park Street, Camberley, in 1964 when Watney's Red Barrel was the tipple of choice at the Carpenters.

Opposite: The Jolly Farmer looking very tranquil (closed) in the 1960s. Its triangle has gone in favour of a roundabout now.

The Fighting Cocks pub, Bagshot, in the early 1960s. The A30 was the main connecting road between London and the South West then. In the old 'ton-up' days, motor-cyclists would assemble in the car park here and charge off to the triangle outside the Jolly Farmer, aiming to hit the 100 mph mark on the way back.

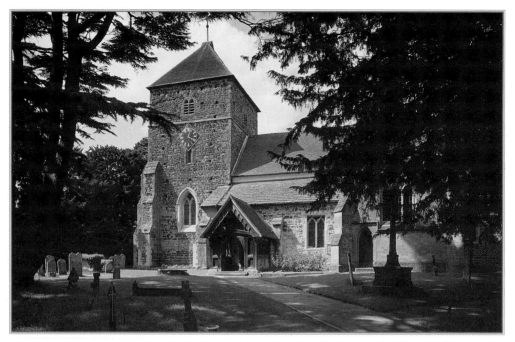

The parish church of St Nicholas at Cranleigh was heavily restored in the mid-nineteenth century. The holes in the tower are not for pigeons, but are the 'putlogs' for the original scaffolding.

Cranleigh – it changed its name from Craneley in 1876 at the request of the Post Office, to avoid confusion with Crawley – claims to be the biggest village in England. The Wey to Arun Navigation runs behind these buildings in the High Street and the Onslow Arms is the starting point for narrow boat trips.

The Fountain was given to the village by the Bradshaws of Knowle in memory of their son, Arthur.

Here's a wider view of the Fountain and the surrounding area in the mid-1960s.

Cranleigh and the nearby Vachery Pond were centres for Wealden ironworking in the distant past. More recently bricks were made here and transported by barge to London and beyond.

The name
Chiddingfold means
the 'fold' – animal
enclosure – in the
hollow. Four
thousand of
Edward VI's men
encamped on the
Green in 1552.

Edward himself put up at the Crown Inn. Built on the site of the Saxon halle, this is believed to have been built by Cistercian monks as an inn in 1285. For many years the building appeared more modern, having been tile-hung from sometime in the late seventeenth century. Its ancient half-timbered façade was revealed in the course of repair work in 1951.

Opposite: Two views of St Mary's church at Chiddingfold in the 1960s. Built in the thirteenth century, it was restored in 1869. The west window of the south aisle is made up of glass fragments from the local furnaces that used to abound here. The village's glass-making fame was brought to an end after over 300 years, when the locals petitioned Queen Elizabeth I, claiming it was a nuisance to them.

The Pride of the Valley Hotel at Churt. Now a popular wedding venue and the setting for music festivals, it has sixteen suites, each with a different theme.

Caravanning and camping continue to be the most popular form of tourism in the British Isles. This is Symondstone Farm at Churt in the 1970s.

St Andrew's church in Cobham is a fine example of the use of puddingstone – a conglomeration of flint and sandstone in iron oxide cement.

Opposite: Church Stile House has passed through various hands. A brewer by the name of Bellow gave it to the parish of Clerkenwell in 1614 on condition that 20s from its rent be distributed to the poor on each Good Friday. It remained in their possession for about three hundred years. It is believed to date back to 1432, though it was restored in 1635. In 1902 it was used by a Miss Blunt as a house of rest for ladies of insufficient means and a school for crippled children. It reverted to private use in 1948.

The first mention of The Running Mare at Cobham is from 1756, though it is believed to have existed previously. Its name is thought to be unique in England.

You're never far from water in Cobham. Built in a loop of the River Mole, it is surrounded on three sides.

Nowadays Croydon is part of the London sprawl which has been absorbing bits of
Surrey ever since the first cab driver agreed to go 'south of the river'. It is believed
originally to have been a Roman staging post and gets its name from the Saxon for
'crooked valley'. The parish church is mainly fifteenth century, though it was extensively
rebuilt following a fire in 1867.

Opposite: Croydon Town Hall in Katharine Street in the 1930s. This grand building
opened in 1896 as part of one of Croydon's frequent 'redevelopments'. The previous
town hall had been demolished in 1808 in an earlier one. The 'London Borough of
Croydon' set up in Taberner House in 1967.

Fairfield Halls opened in 1962 and brought concert-going into the rock age. Some very young Rolling Stones played there as part of their first UK tour on 7 December of that year.

Dorking gets its name from a Saxon word for a small common or heath. The writer
J.C. Cox, visiting in around 1908, had this to say: 'The High Street, with its slight
curvature and with its raised causeway on the south side, still retains a pleasing variety
of houses, only two or three of which are in any sense vulgar or offensive.'

Opposite: Croydon Aerodrome was officially opened on 29 March 1920. Formed from
two First World War airfields, it was unusual in being divided by a road – Plough Lane.
A 'level crossing' was made and motorists were held up by a man with a flag (later a
gate) when planes needed to cross. In 1930 Amy Johnson flew from here on her historic
flight to Australia. The two new planes here belong to Olley Air Service, which
commenced flights from Croydon in 1934. They are De Havilland DH.84 Dragons, and
the one in front seems to be aircraft G-ACNA, registered to Olley as number 6068.

A corner of old
Dorking.

The White Horse, seen opposite in the 1960s, was known as the Cross House until 1750 and dates back a further 300 years.

There have been several parish churches at Dorking since the one recorded in the Domesday Book. Completed in 1877, the spire of the present St Martin's was less than forty years old when this photograph was taken.

The image of tranquillity one hundred years ago, and much the same today, Friday Street, near Dorking, once played its part in local industries, when the Tillingbourne Valley rang with the workings of iron, cloth and gunpowder mills. It is well known in the region for the Stephen Langton pub-restaurant, which was named after King John's Archbishop of Canterbury, who was born in Friday Street in 1150 and played a major part in drawing up the Magna Carta.

Another idyllic scene
from the beginning of
the last century. Castle
Mill has been a
subject for painters
and photographers for
generations.

The presence of the Woolpack pub gives a good indication of the origins of Elstead, although the village's name refers to the elder trees that grew there. It is now known for having some of the best preserved heathland in England – much of it within the area now under the control of the Ministry of Defence, the ancient commons common no more, though walkers are permitted within the boundaries at agreed times. Elstead church was restored and enlarged in 1872.

At heart, Epsom is, or was, a sleepy market town. It had greatness thrust upon it in two periods of its history – once when the legendary Epsom Salts were discovered in the seventeenth century; the second time a century later when the Earl of Derby founded his famous horse race on the downs. Throughout the eighteenth century it was a fashionable resort, though now the source of the salts is seldom visited and, when the occasional coach trip does turn up, it causes traffic chaos in The Greenway. These pictures, all angles on the unmistakable Victorian clock tower, were taken in the 1960s.

Rosebery Park now incorporates the town's sports ground. Between 1899 and 1924 no fewer than five mental hospitals were built in and around Epsom. Most were later demolished and their grounds returned to parkland.

Opposite: The Spread Eagle at Epsom in the early and late 1960s. The first picture, with the Vauxhall Wyvern outside the door, is from around 1962, with Reid's furniture, carpet and bedding store and Reynold's estate agency alongside. The later shot is from around 1968 – the new Euro-road signs and 'symbolic' keep left signs are in place. The artist Aubrey Beardsley lived in Epsom as a child and returned to stay in the Spread Eagle in his declining years. Nowadays the Eagle is home to horse-racing and top-people's outfitter, Lester Bowden's store.

Epsom racecourse photographed between the wars. This recalls the time when race meetings were also fairs for gypsies and horse-traders. *Inset*: The racecourse in the 1970s. The grandstand has been somewhat redeveloped, mainly to house television commentators and equipment, but remains substantially the same as in the earlier picture.

The old parish church of St George at Esher dates back to 1540. It was abandoned when the new church was built in 1834, although it contained a unique three-deck pulpit and a double-chamber pew. The Bear, whose sign can be seen to the left of this early 1960s photograph, is even older, having been established as a coaching inn in 1529. King Louis Philippe of France died in exile at nearby Claremont House and was a frequent visitor to the Bear.

The church at Fernhurst, like St Margaret's at Westminster, is dedicated to St Margaret of Antioch – a favourite saint of the Crusaders and visitors to the Holy Land. It was probably built by soldiers in the twelfth century.

Opposite: Farnham Castle was built in 1138 by the grandson of William the Conqueror, Henri de Blois. For the next 800 years it was the home of the Bishops of Winchester who, judging by the old Peugeot 403 in this 1960s picture, maintained some of their French leanings. For the last half-century the castle has been the home of the Farnham Castle International Briefing and Conference Centre.

Bertrand Russell lived at Fernhurst (at Vann Bridge Cottage) so much philosophising took place in the village in the nineteenth century. The little antiques shop in this picture is now a printing works. I wonder what he'd make of that.

Opposite: Frimley Green retains the landmark that gave it its name along with some quite ancient houses. 'Frimley' itself derives from Fremma's lea, or meadow. The Lakeside Country Club is now a nearby attraction.

The church of St Andrew at Frimley Green was opened on 27 April 1912 as a result of the efforts of local parishioners, and replaced a 'tin church' which had served the community for the previous quarter century. Tin churches were a kind of basic ecclesiastical prefab that served in extremis. In 1962 St Andrew's became the church for the new enlarged parish of Frimley Green and Mytchett.

Norman in origin, the parish church of St Peter and St Paul at Godalming has been
extensively restored at various times – so badly in 1840 that Sir Gilbert Scott had to be
brought in in 1879 to undo and redo it. The picture on the left was taken in the 1930s,
not many years after the removal of a gigantic tree that obscured and threatened the
houses on the right. *Above*: Thirty-odd years later and not much has changed.
The graceful street lamp has been replaced by a vulgar angular affair. In the place of the
Morris and Riley are Morrises, Fords, a Vauxhall and an Austin A40.

Cloth and paper built modern Godalming, though
it was a royal hunting resort for the centuries from
its bequest by Alfred the Great to his nephew
Ethelwald to the Restoration. Known locally as
'The Pepperpot', the Market Hall was built by
public subscription in 1814. Once open to traders,
later railed off, by the time of this photograph it
had become a local museum. The museum has now
moved across the road.

Whitehall in Mint Street dates from around 1500. This photograph was taken in the 1940s.

The Anchor Inn
in Ockford Road,
also in the 1940s.
Godalming stands
at the junction of
the Wey and the
Ock.

Once a hive of industry, Eashing is now the ideal vision of a quiet backwater. These are the houses known as The Meads. The timber framing is from the sixteenth century. The photo is from around 1909.

Great Bookham, birthplace in 1943 of Pink Floyd's Roger Waters. Here are the post office and Lipton's grocery shop a couple of years before Arnold Layne's strange habit was first revealed to the world in March 1967.

Ye Olde Windsor Castle near Bookham station is as 'olde' as it claims to be, dating as it does from the sixteenth century.

Opposite: Both Fanny Burney and Jane Austen worshipped at Great Bookham's parish church of St Nicholas. It is believed there was a church here as far back as the fifth century. One certainly existed at the time of Domesday. The Slyfield Chapel was added in 1440 and once had a private entrance, the outline of which is still visible.

The Archbishop of Canterbury laid the first stone for the Cathedral of the Holy Spirit – the first Anglican cathedral to be built on a new location since the Reformation – in July 1936. The Second World War got in the way of its construction three years later. Here it is part completed, its tower temporarily capped with a weatherproof wooden structure.

Opposite: Here is the cathedral following completion and consecration in 1961. It was designed by Sir Edward Maufe. Set on the summit of Stag Hill, it holds a commanding position above Surrey's county town. In those days it stood alone. Now its once sacred lands have been sold off to housing developers and even accommodate one of the grosser kinds of international hotel.

A telephoto shot of the Golden Angel weathervane. When it needed regilding recently, a mobile phone operator covered the cost in return for its use as an aerial.

These interior views of the cathedral capture
the success with which the clean but imposing
lines of the exterior have been carried inside.
Less is more here where, by comparison with
Coventry or Liverpool, simple but towering
modern-gothic spaces have been decorated on a
human scale.

The name 'Gyldeforda' meant 'golden crossing'. This is Guildford's High Street and seventeenth-century Guildhall in the 1920s. In those days all through traffic came this way.

The planners in Guildford seem to have had a propensity for suspending large objects above the heads of pedestrians. This appears to be the entrance to the Angel – an old coaching inn that now fronts a shopping centre. Clark's Limited would not get away with that rooftop sign today.

The story goes that clockmaker John Aylward was refused permission to open a shop in Guildford. He presented this fine clock to the town and the powers-that-be could no longer be churlish.

Opposite: When Guildford's bypass was first opened, you really could get away from it all. Racing driver Mike Hawthorn died in a car crash here in 1959.

Guildford Castle appears tame these days. It was probably built in the reign of Henry II.
King John was a frequent incumbent and it was seized in 1216 by Louis, Dauphin of
France. It was put up for sale in 1885 and acquired by the town.

Castle Arch formerly led to the King's private quarters. It was built by John of
Gloucester in 1256. This picture is from about 1905.

The same view in the 1970s reveals some doubtful 'antiquing' of the house on the far
side of Quarry Street.

An early 1900s picture of Rosemary Alley, previously known, according to Arthur Mee, as Old Porridgepot Alley. It is actually more likely that it was Old Pomage Pot – referring to the bakery shops and groceries that existed here, pomage being the term for a kind of cooking fat. Running from Quarry Street – the old coach road for Portsmouth – to the Yvonne Arnaud Theatre, it was in recent years the subject of vital lighting improvements.

South Street led off Sydenham Road and connected it to Castle Street, where Lewis
Carroll used to stay. This picture from around 1905 recalls another world.

These parts of Guildford were regarded as old then. The figure at the upstairs casement
in the picture opposite has a particularly haunting quality.

The Old Quarry stood at the edge of Guildford on the Horsham side.

The Yvonne Arnaud Theatre opened in 1965 in honour of the French actress who made her home at Effingham Common and who graced the English stage for forty-six years. This photograph celebrated its completion.

Opposite: Many towns had their equivalent of the pesthouse or later isolation hospital before the days of drugs. The Pilgrims' Way has always been popular with tourists. It is not recorded how many people sent postcards from the pesthouse.

The Britannia
in Mill Lane.
The pub name
still exists,
though the area
is now called
Mill Mead.

Halfway between Guildford and Chichester, Haslemere has been a market town since 1394. An ex-member of parliament, General James Edward Oglethorpe, founded the colony of Georgia.

The war memorial in Haslemere in quieter times.

Opposite: Haslemere got its name from the hazel trees that surrounded the lake or 'mere' that once occupied the area between Derby Road and the High Street.

Haslemere in the late 1960s. The White Horse is an old coaching inn and a music venue.

Shepherd's Hill, Haslemere, between the wars . . .

. . . and in the late 1960s. Not much has changed. The streetlights are uglier, the dotted line is more joined-up. Where nobody would park, nobody can park, and the rooftops have sprouted aerials. The houses date from the sixteenth century.

Hindhead's shops and dwellings grew up around the local attractions of the head itself and the Devil's Punchbowl – both within such easy reach of the old London to Portsmouth coach route that became the A3.

This view from the top of Gibbet Hill in the 1970s could have been taken at any time in the last 100 years or more.

Opposite: The Celtic cross erected in 1851 on the site of the old gibbet near the rim of the Devil's Punchbowl.

Opposite: This picture of the Old Portsmouth Road from the same time gives an indication of how desolate the countryside could be for a lone traveller in those days.

The Broomsquire's Cottage at Hindhead in 1905. This was the setting for the novel *The Broomsquire* published in 1896 by Exeter-born writer Sabine Baring-Gould, based on the actual murder of a sailor by three men on Hindhead Common in 1786. The book was extremely popular when this photograph was taken and would go on to a tenth edition by the end of the First World War.

Horley is not mentioned in Domesday, but is recorded as a manor under the control of
the Benedictine Abbey of St Peter at Chertsey in Saxon times. This shows the junction of
the High Street with Albert Road in the 1960s.

Ye Olde Six Bells has been called that since 1393, having already been there for at least
ninety years. It was at the heart of one of the three hamlets that eventually formed
Horley. Its garden backs on to the River Mole.

St Bartholomew's church has windows dating from the fourteenth century, though the appearance of the building has experienced some major 'renovations'. One, in 1881, was considered so 'grievous' that a second to undo the wrong was undertaken in around 1900.

Now very much part of
London, Kingston-upon-
Thames was historically one
of the most important towns
in Surrey. Its name refers to
the Saxon Coronation Stone.

The growth of Kingston originated from the fact that this was the lowest point where it was possible to ford the Thames. Alfred the Great held his Great Council here in 838 and it was described as 'that famous place called Kingston in Surrey'.

There has been a Kingston Bridge since Saxon times. Early versions were of wood and, until 1750, when Westminster Bridge was built, were the next crossing up-river to London Bridge. Designed by Edward Lapidge, the present bridge is actually two. The original, built in 1828, was widened in 1914 by building a 'duplicate' with a similar façade. It currently carries in excess of 50,000 vehicles a day.

Opposite: The first Norman church was begun in around 1120, using recycled bits of the previous Saxon one. The present All Saints' dates from the thirteenth century.

Leith Hill is the highest point in south-east England. No fewer than twelve counties can
be seen from its summit. The tower is the work of Richard Hull and dates from 1766.
Hull himself is buried beneath the floor.

Lingfield in the 1960s. The church of St Peter and St Paul was rebuilt in 1431, though the tower is a hundred years older. It is the only large church in the Perpendicular style in Surrey. The town is best known for its race meetings which occur every month. The larger picture is of the 'old cage', a tiny gaol, built in 1773. Its last inmate was released in 1882. The pub named after it was there in 1590. I recall being there myself in the late 1970s, though I don't remember leaving.

The A25 at Limpsfield. A lot has changed around here in the thirty-plus years since this photograph was taken. The church of St Peter, relatively untroubled since the twelfth century, now gazes at Titsey Hill across the M25. The composer Frederick Delius is buried in its churchyard.

Opposite: Limpsfield High Street in the 1970s. The parish stretches 6 miles north to south and hugs the A25 on both sides for more than 2 miles. It incorporates the hamlets of Pains Hill, Langhurst and Moorhouse, the last named marking the border with Kent.

St Mary's church at Oxted once had a spire on top of its fifteenth-century tower.

Opposite: Two miles from Guildford, Merrow stands on the edge of parkland originally laid out by Capability Brown. Although containing many Norman elements, the church was pulled down and rebuilt in 1842. The Horse and Groom inn next door dates back to 1615.

Oxted in the 1970s when the A25 ran through the middle of the town. Now it has been bypassed while it still retains enough of its character.

The parish church of St Mary Magdalene at Reigate. Originally built between the twelfth and fifteenth centuries, it was much restored in the mid-nineteenth.

Richmond in Surrey got its name from Richmond in Yorkshire, thanks to Henry VII
(whose father was the Earl of Richmond), who changed it from Sheen because he could.
Richmond Bridge was designed by James Paine and Kenton Couse, and was opened in
January 1777.

Opposite: Two sides of the Market House or Old Town Hall in Reigate at the beginning
and end of the 1960s. Built in 1708, it stands on the site of a shrine to St Thomas of
Canterbury, which was ruined during the Reformation.

Shere in the
early years of
the twentieth
century.
Sanders &
Sons were
among the first
businesses in
the village to
be motorised.

Shere's Norman church has a medieval shingled spire and a spooky history. The daughter of one William the Carpenter, by the name of Christine, lived in a cell in the north wall from 1329. Pilgrims used to come and observe her, and she was able to follow services in the church via a 'squint'. She was described as a hermit, and was known as the Anchoress or Anchorite, from the Greek for 'one who lives in seclusion'. However, the fact that she broke out in the early 1330s and had to be re-enclosed suggests that this might have conflicted somewhat with her self-image.

Opposite: Surbiton comes from 'suth-bere-tun' – a southern farm or barn. Perhaps the most notable feature in these two pictures of the town is the omnipresence of overhead cables, originally put there by the United Tramways Company in around 1908. No tramlines are visible here, so they would have progressed to powering trolleybuses.

St Mark's is one of two parish churches in Surbiton (the other is St Andrew's). It was
built between 1845 and 1960, so was newly completed when this photograph
was taken.

Raven's Ait is a mecca for yachtsmen, film-makers and those bent on matrimony. 'Ait' is the name used for a small island hereabouts. It is sometimes spelt 'eyot' and owes a lot to the French 'îlot'.

Queen's Promenade has been a fashionable walkway for generations where the Thames runs alongside the Portsmouth Road. Hampton Court is on the opposite bank.

Opposite: The parish church of St Nicholas at Thames Ditton was, before 1769, a chapel in the parish of Kingston. Built on a Norman foundation, it has been extended over the centuries, the last time in 1995. In its churchyard is the grave of 'La Belle Pamela', daughter of the Duc d'Orleans and wife of Lord Henry Fitzgerald, who lived in Thames Ditton. She died in Montmartre but was returned here for burial.

Ye Olde Swan is still providing succour to the imbibers of Thames Ditton, though it no longer claims to have a thirteenth-century car park. The decidedly mid-twentieth-century Truman's Beer sign has also been judiciously done away with.

Opposite: AC Cars, maker of the legendary Cobra sports cars, was based in Thames Ditton from 1911 to 1980. They also made the 'Petite' three-wheelers that formed the basis of Britain's 'invalid carriages', one of which is visible in the photograph of Oxted. Looking very 'villagey' in these 1960s shots, Thames Ditton was to suffer from speculative development in later years.

Thursley village before the First World War. During that war the landlady of the Three
Horseshoes allegedly supplied women to the Canadian soldiers. The brewery didn't
share her view of what constituted hospitality, so had her replaced.

Virginia Water was created in the parish of Egham in 1746 by then deputy-ranger of
Windsor Park, Thomas Sandby. One and a half miles long by about half a mile in width,
it is not all in Surrey, parts of it reaching over the border into Berkshire.

The actor Leslie Howard (star of *Intermezzo* and *Gone with the Wind*) lived in Westcott. He died when his British Overseas Airways plane was shot down by the enemy over the Bay of Biscay in June 1943 as he was returning from Portugal. The Crown Inn has been an ale house since the fifteenth century. These pictures are from the 1950s.

You don't have to be my age to think of Weybridge as the location of the Labour Exchange, manned by Henry McGhee, to which Charlie Drake's *The Worker* reported following his defection from the BBC. The first series might have been in 1965, but the last was in 1978. Weybridge is at the confluence of the Wey and the Thames. It is perhaps best known for the production of aircraft. The ferry is crossing toward Ferry Lane on the Shepperton side and a building belonging to George Dunton, boatbuilder. Nauticalia is now on the northern bank.

Wimbledon church was rebuilt in 1778
and again in 1843, though there are
traces of earlier elements from the
fourteenth and fifteenth centuries.

Long before Elisabeth
Beresford and the Wombles
there were hut dwellers on
Wimbledon Common, very
near to the windmill seen
here in the 1920s. Their hut
circles were discovered
seventy years before. The
area was long known as
Caesar's camp, but was
actually of Celtic
construction.

Putney Bridge in 1905. Famous the world over as the starting point for the Oxford and Cambridge Boat Race, the present granite structure was built in 1886. The previous – wooden – Putney Bridge was built in 1729.

Arthur's Bridge over the canal at Woking before the First World War. Nowadays it's restricted to pedestrian traffic.

The Shah Jahan Mosque in Woking dates from 1889, and was the first to be built in the UK. It was conceived by a Hungarian called Gottlieb Leitner who wanted to create an academy for oriental studies. He built the mosque next door to the Royal Dramatic College – a home for retired actors.

Newark Priory was built during the reign of Richard the Lionheart. From the thirteenth to the sixteenth centuries its canons controlled Woking.

You could push a pram about in Guildford Road, Woking, now part of the A320, in the early years of the twentieth century. It would not be advisable to do it now.

The village of Wotton is no longer with us, though this Norman church can still be found just off the A25 near Dorking.